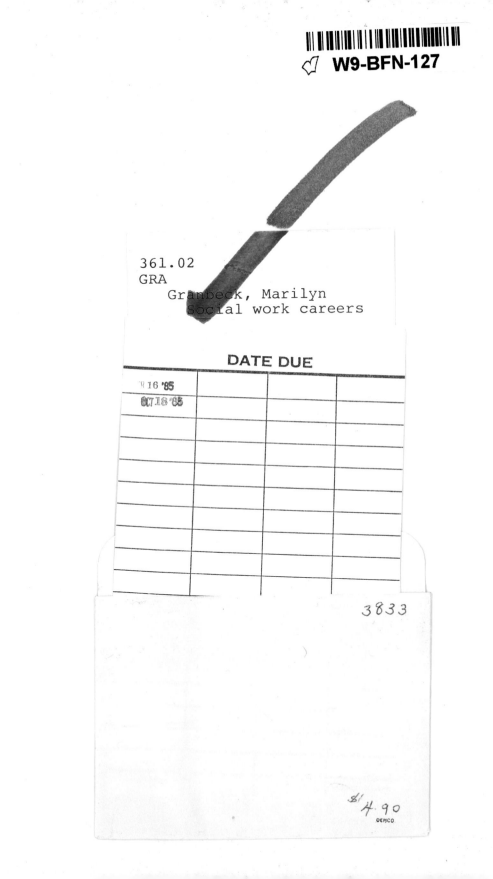

SOCIAL WORK CAREERS

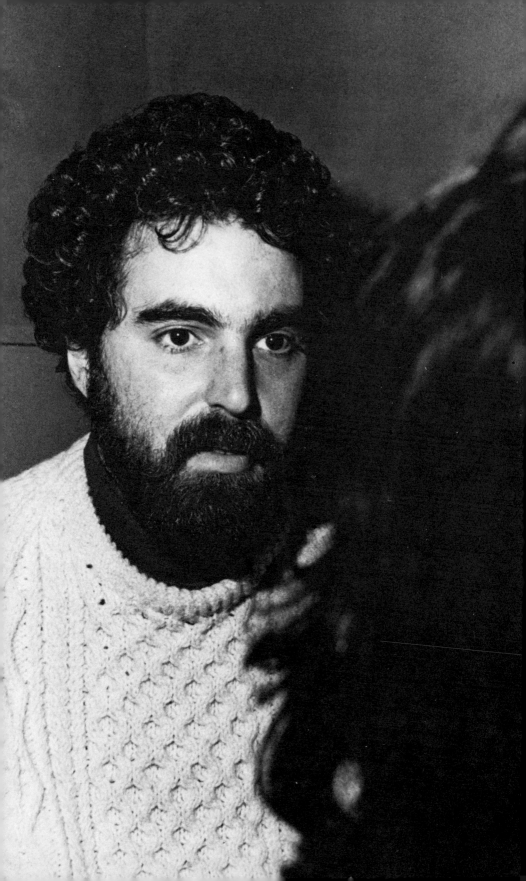

SOCIAL WORK CAREERS

by Marilyn Granbeck

PHOTOGRAPHS BY
CHUCK FREEDMAN

A Career Concise Guide

FRANKLIN WATTS
NEW YORK | LONDON | 1977

Acknowledgments
Joel Edelstein and Ramon Rueda of People's De-
velopment Corporation; Armand DiMele and Susan
Shor of The DiMele Center for Reconnective
Psychotherapy; Susan Samuel of The New York
Philanthropic League; Teresa Guardian of St.
Luke's Hospital, Department of Social Services;
Dr. and Mrs. Charles Rohrs; Arthur Totman; and
Daniel Agostini of Aspira.

Photograph on page 51 courtesy of ACTION

Library of Congress Cataloging in Publication Data

Granbeck, Marilyn.
    Social work careers.

    (A Career concise guide)
    Includes index.
    SUMMARY: Discusses various jobs in the
field of social work. Includes family counselor, psychiatric social worker, parole agent, and fund
raiser.
    1. Social service—Vocational guidance—
Juvenile literature. [1. Social service—Vocational
guidance. 2. Vocational guidance] I. Title.
HV10.5.G7   361'.0023   77-6456
ISBN 0-531-01310-3

3833

Contents

This book is dedicated to
Kanata Wilson and Grant Shepard

SOCIAL WORK CAREERS

Introduction

Men and women are social beings, born into a world of people with whom they live, study, work, and eventually die. Their ability to think and plan sets them apart from other animals. They develop personalities and attitudes, decide on careers, places to live, people to be with. At times they may choose solitude, but they are never completely away from the influence of others or their dependency on them. When they encounter problems, they try to solve them so life can go on. Sometimes they may need others to help them solve problems.

Social work is a profession based on the human concern for the well-being of others. It supplies resources and aid so people can help themselves. In general terms, social work is concerned with helping people to solve some of the problems that prevent them from leading normal, happy, productive lives.

Social services exist in almost every city and town in the United States and Canada. They deal with poverty, racial tensions, illness, and hostility, and they touch the lives of almost everyone at some time or other. Social work is fast becoming one of the largest service professions in the world; it provides career opportunities for men and women with a variety of personal and educational backgrounds.

Education

Some social workers have bachelor's degrees (BSW). The professional social worker has a master's degree (MSW), and may have a doctorate (DSW). All of these people are eligible for membership in the National Association of Social Workers (NASW) or the Canadian Association of Social Work. These are professional organizations dedicated to developing high standards and sound policies in social work.

College education in social work gives the student a beginning knowledge of some of the kinds of social services. Graduates may then select fields that interest them most and continue to learn through experience on the job. Employers sometimes provide the opportunity for workers to continue schooling by allowing time off and the incentive of advancement and higher salaries. For example, a BSW can expect to earn $8,000 to $16,000 a year; for an MSW, the salary range is usually between $10,000 and $20,000, depending on the size and location of the agency and the worker's experience. DSWs often reach top positions and may earn salaries up to $50,000 a year. Since times and needs change, all social workers must be willing to attend seminars, read widely, and keep up with new developments.

A hospital doctor, who is also a psychlatric intern, interviews a child at home at the request of a social worker.

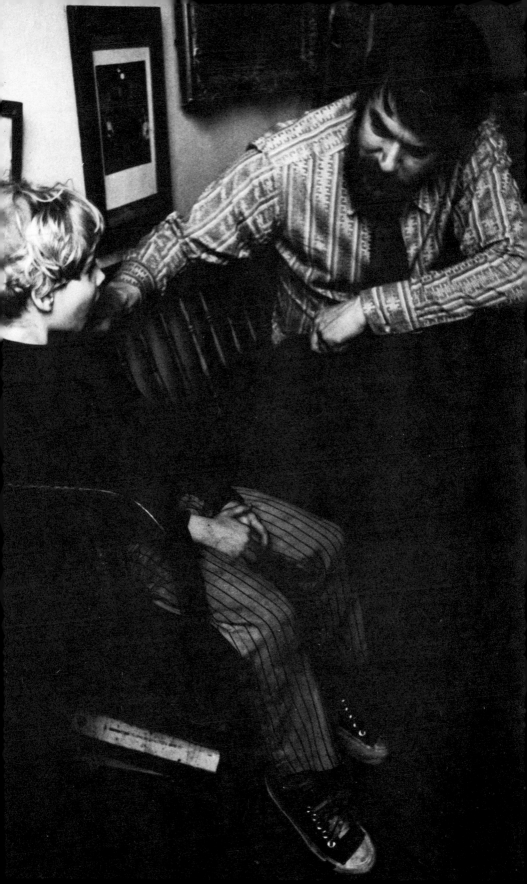

Some social workers stay in one type of service throughout their careers, while others do not. There are advantages to both practices. Caseworkers who spend their entire careers in medical social work, for example, can rise to the top of their profession. A person who likes variety, or wants to gain experience in more than one area of social work, may want to work for several years in different areas such as the fields of public welfare, family counseling, and youth group work. Such a well-rounded background may lead to administrative work or private practice.

Paraprofessionals also play an important role in social services. Paraprofessionals do not usually have college degrees and do not belong to NASW or the Canadian Association of Social Work, but they can join other organizations pertaining to their fields. Paraprofessionals work in jobs that help professional social workers.

There are many colleges and universities at which you can prepare for a career in social work. Free lists are available by writing:

Council on Social Work Education
345 East 46th Street
New York, N.Y. 10017

Canadian Association of Schools
of Social Work
151 Slater Street
Ottawa, Ontario, Canada K1P 5H3

For information on schools for paraprofessional training, write:

National Association
of Trade & Technical Schools
2021 L Street, N.W.
Washington, D.C. 20036

Association
of Independent Colleges & Schools
1730 M Street, N.W.
Washington, D.C. 20036

American Association
of Community and Junior Colleges
1 Dupont Circle, N.W.
Washington, D.C. 20036

Canadian Association
of Social Service Course Directors
1385 Woodroffe Avenue, Block E
Ottawa, Ontario K2G IV 8

Financial aid for careers in social work may be obtained from individual schools, or by writing:

National Commission
for Social Work Careers
2 Park Avenue
New York, N.Y. 10016

Canadian Association
of Schools of Social Work
151 Slater Street
Ottawa, Ontario, K1P 5H3

Social Caseworkers

Since social work is a service profession, it often operates effectively on a one-to-one basis because individuals and families have many kinds of problems for which there is no single solution. The person-to-person approach is called casework, and caseworkers make up a large proportion of people in this profession.

Casework is the oldest method of social work. It involves workers closely with clients and lets them concentrate on particular needs and difficulties. Caseworkers must be good listeners and have the ability to see beyond surface complaints in order to get at the roots of problems. They must be familiar with the social services that the city, county, state, or province provides so that they can refer clients to sources of additional help.

Salaries for caseworkers depend on the size of the agency and the size of the city where it's located. Most caseworkers earn between $9,000 (BSW) and $18,000 (experienced MSW) a year. Paraprofessionals earn $6,000 to $8,000 a year or may be paid on an hourly basis, from $2.40 to $4.00. In general, Canadian salaries are comparable to those in the United States, sometimes slightly higher. Most agencies offer fringe benefits such as sick leave, paid vacations, and group insurance.

CHILD WELFARE WORKER

Charlotte MacRoy works in the child protection services of a county public welfare office and is on call twenty-four hours a day seven days a week. If a policeman, sheriff, or fireman encounters a case of child abuse or neglect, an emergency number will reach Charlotte. Late one night she was called to pick up a neglected child. Neighbors called the police when they heard four-year-old Rachel crying, and suspected that the child's mother had left her alone, something that had happened several times before. When police entered the apartment they found Rachel hungry, dirty, and frightened.

This was not the first time Charlotte had picked up Rachel on an emergency call. Last year Rachel was in a foster home for three months while Charlotte counseled the mother, Dorothy. Charlotte sent Dorothy to a clinic for

A social worker checks on reports she has received concerning the welfare of a child in a rural area.

alcoholics so that she could try to solve her drinking problem. She helped her find a part-time job and arranged for a babysitter for Rachel. She also helped Dorothy work out a healthy diet and a food budget. She even showed Dorothy how to clean and cook. Now, Charlotte wondered if any of her counseling had done much good. The apartment was a mess, Rachel looked thin and sick, and neighbors reported frequent fights between Dorothy and drinking companions.

Charlotte took Rachel to a foster home and put her to bed. The next morning she prepared the papers necessary for the hearing to make Rachel a ward of the court, so that she could be kept in a foster home until her case was settled. Rachel and Dorothy are both Charlotte's clients. Now the counseling process will begin all over again.

Caseworkers in child welfare provide many kinds of help to protect children. They work with children who come from broken homes, are born out of wedlock, get in trouble with the law, or are beaten or abused by their families. They work with children with emotional, physical, or mental handicaps, and those whose parents are unable to provide proper homes. They also handle adoptions and supervise children in foster homes.

Another important part of a child welfare agent's work is with minor unwed mothers. The decision to keep the child or place it for adoption is a difficult one to make, and the caseworker tries to give the mother-to-be information and guidance that will help her decide wisely. Whether the girl keeps the baby or gives it up, the caseworker continues to help her in every possible way. After the baby is born, the child and the mother continue to be clients of the caseworker, who works in their best interests.

A child welfare worker must know the resources of the community. Charlotte may help the family of a mentally retarded youngster by arranging visits to private and state institutions so that they can see what kind of care is given there. She may suggest special schools or training centers or direct the family to counseling services that will help them determine the child's capabilities and what programs will help most. She may also put them in touch with groups for families with retarded children.

A child welfare worker also helps youngsters by arranging for them to go to camp or join youth groups that provide social contacts and the chance to learn new skills. In many areas, volunteers work as tutors and companions to children with problems, and the caseworker brings children and volunteers together.

Both men and women hold jobs as child welfare workers. An MSW is required in almost all public and private agencies for this job, although some agencies do employ people with BA degrees.

FAMILY COUNSELOR

Carl and Audrey Stevens have been married ten years, but they are unhappy. Carl has been out of work for almost a year, and recently he suffered a broken leg in a car accident. He's borrowed money from friends and relatives, run up bills at stores, and owes last month's rent on the family apartment. Audrey works as a waitress but her paycheck doesn't stretch to pay the bills and buy food and clothing for eight-year-old Greta and four-year-old Paul. Audrey and Carl argue often. Audrey is irritable and talks about divorce. A friend suggests a family counselor.

Dean Walker is a family counselor with the county department of social services. When he is assigned as Audrey's caseworker, he listens and encourages her to express her feelings. Dean knows that under her anger and frustration, Audrey is confused and worried. If some

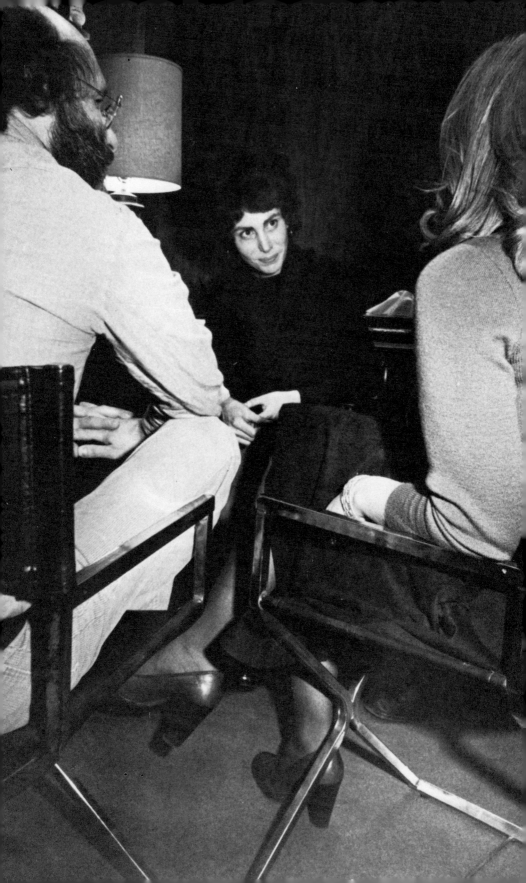

of the responsibility can be lifted from her shoulders, maybe Audrey can cope. Mostly, she needs to know that she is not struggling alone.

Dean talks with Carl and meets Greta and Paul. At first Carl is angry, but when he realizes that Dean is not offering charity but friendly assistance, his attitude changes. He tells Dean he is worried about not having a job; Audrey is so tired when she comes home from work that she finds fault because he hasn't started supper or cleaned the apartment; taking care of a lively four-year-old puts Carl under a strain, and he's fallen into the habit of yelling when the kids do not do what he tells them.

Greta resents her father's moods and the fact that she has to watch her brother after school, so she does not come home until supper time, and she pouts when her mother demands help. Little Paul is bored and restless at not being allowed outside because his father can't watch him, so he smashes toys, writes on walls, and hides.

The first thing Dean does is help Audrey and Carl work out a budget. He tells them they can apply for food stamps and where to do this. By spending less on food, there will be enough to pay the rent and some of the other bills. Dean talks to the landlord who agrees to wait for the money. He also says he needs a caretaker, and offers the job to Carl as soon as he can get around. Dean tells Carl about free classes at a nearby adult education center. With training, Carl may be able to get another type of job. Dean also arranges for a homemaking-health aide to come twice a week and help plan menus, clean

A husband and wife visit a marriage counselor at the Di Mele Center for Reconnective Psychotherapy for help with their family problems.

the apartment, and show Greta and Carl easy dinners they can cook. Finally, he arranges for Paul to attend a nursery school several hours each afternoon, so that Carl can have time to relax.

Family counselors work for public and private agencies. They serve families, but they may also handle practical arrangements for individual members as well. Marriage counseling, conflicts between parents and children, problems with aged parents, guidance and assistance for families troubled by illness or poverty are dealt with in this job.

The Red Cross uses assistant field directors to counsel families of servicemen and veterans. Churches operate counseling services, as do community and mental health centers. An MSW is required for most jobs in family counseling.

HOMEMAKING-HEALTH AIDE

The homemaking-health aide is a paraprofessional and does not have special training. One of the newest ideas in social service is helping people live at home instead of going to an institution. The federal government pays for a Homemaker Chore program, which many states operate under their Departments of Public Social Service.

A homemaking-health aide is assigned to a client by the caseworker. An elderly woman living alone who can cook and tend her personal needs might require a homemaker once a week to vacuum and wash floors. A man on crutches may need help shampooing his hair or taking a bath. Someone else may be able to do all these things but cannot shop for groceries or plan a good diet.

The aide visits a client anywhere from once a day to once a month, depending on the need. He or she is paid by the hour, and aides are often recruited from poverty areas or are people on welfare, but this is not a requirement for the job. You can get information about this job from your local Department of Social Services.

SCHOOL SOCIAL WORKER

Youngsters spend a lot of time in school, and problems often show up there before they are noticed elsewhere. A child who has been doing well suddenly begins failing. A child recently transferred from another school plays truant. Why?

Many school systems employ school social workers to cooperate with teachers and principals in solving these problems. A school social worker may work for one school or for several in a district. Since each child is different, there is no set approach to this casework. Jean Carver usually begins by talking to the teacher who first noticed the problem. Then she talks to the child and tries to gain his trust; at the same time she watches for clues to the cause of the trouble. The problem may be as simple as a misunderstanding or clash of personalities between student and teacher that can be worked out by counseling or changing the classroom. But many difficulties stem from home problems, and when they do, Jean visits the home and includes the family in her counseling. She also asks parents to come to school to talk with her.

Peter K.'s mother had to go to work to add to the family income. With no one to get him off to school, Peter was skipping breakfast. He was irritable and tired easily, and it was hard for him to concentrate. He began fighting and causing trouble in class. Jean suggested to Mrs. K. that she arrange Peter's bedtime so that he could get up an hour earlier and eat breakfast with her. Jean let Peter talk about his feelings of rejection. She helped him understand them by explaining that his mother's absence

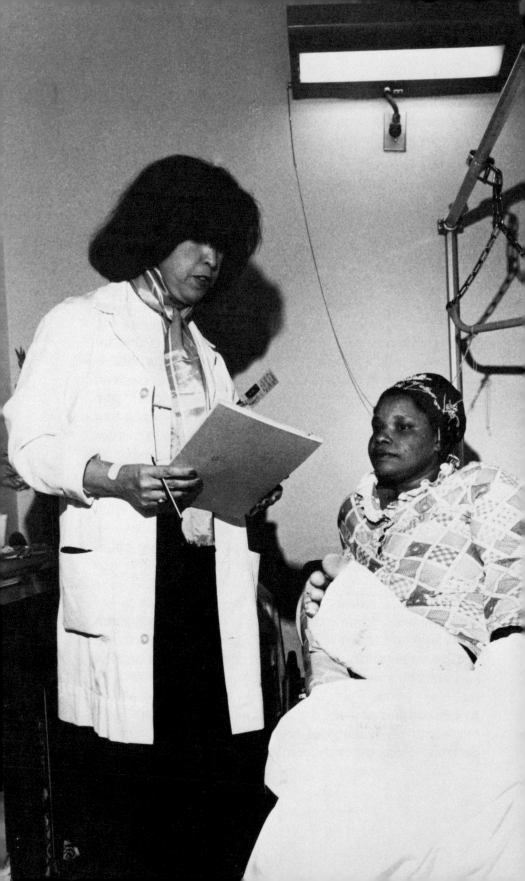

did not mean she didn't love him. Jean suggested that Peter could help his mother by keeping his room clean. She also encouraged him to join a neighborhood boys' club and make new friends. Over a period of months, Jean was rewarded by Peter's smiles when they met at school, and by the news that his work had improved and he was no longer causing trouble.

School social workers also cooperate with school psychiatrists and counselors in testing programs that help to place each youngster in the right class. They work with leaders of the Scouts, Y groups, and other youth associations to provide social contacts and experiences for children. In dealing with truancy or delinquency, they are in touch with probation officers and other law-enforcement persons. They work at both elementary and secondary levels, but not all school systems hire social workers for this specialty.

The Board of Education in your area can supply information. Large city schools usually require an MSW; some smaller communities hire BSWs who have counseling experience.

MEDICAL SOCIAL WORKER

Roger Scarlese has a small, pleasant office in a large hospital in Los Angeles, but he spends much of his time in other parts of the hospital. Each morning he makes ward rounds with staff doctors, listening to discussions of patients' problems. He understands medical terms and treatments, but he is more interested in the human side

To help make arrangements for home care, a social worker from St. Luke's Hospital Department of Social Service visits a patient about to be released.

of patients' troubles. Roger Scarlese is a medical social worker.

Carlos Mendez was recovering from a gall bladder operation and was soon to be discharged from the hospital. Instead of being happy, Carlos was worried and nervous. Roger learned that Carlos lived on the third floor of a rooming house. Carlos was worried about the stairs and how he would get out for meals. He had nowhere else to go, and his pension was too small to pay for a nursing home.

Roger told Carlos his problem could be solved. First, he said that Medicare would cover the cost of a few weeks in a nursing home. Roger described several, and Carlos decided on one not far from his old neighborhood. Roger arranged for Carlos' transfer to the home and promised to find him a new rooming house when he got out.

Medical social workers help families of patients, too. They also comfort the loved ones of patients who are seriously ill, or guide them to useful community services. Sometimes they talk to patients who are nervous before surgery or who do not have any other visitors.

In recent years, many hospitals have established social service departments. Medical social workers may be employed in medical schools to teach nurses and public health personnel. They work in clinics, sanitariums, emergency rooms, and convalescent homes— wherever patients may be facing death or the problems of adjusting to illness or recovery. An MSW is required for medical social work, although some hospitals hire people with BA degrees who are then called social work aides or assistants.

PSYCHIATRIC SOCIAL WORKER

Psychiatric social work is a specialty in the medical

field. Psychiatric social workers deal with problems related to mental health; they are employed in mental hospitals, residential treatment facilities, and mental health clinics. They must understand mental illness, the methods of treatment used in psychiatry, and the social problems that arise in connection with mental illness. They have to be able to relate to the patient, his family, and to the medical staff.

When a patient is hospitalized for mental illness, he or she often does not know or understand what caused the problem. It's the psychiatric social worker's job to learn each patient's family and social background and to contribute this information to the medical treatment team. The caseworker also works directly with patients, answering questions and being willing to talk. The psychiatric social worker helps families understand the nature of the patient's illness and treatment. Sometimes family members need to be aware of the part they play in the illness, and the social worker counsels them or recommends agencies where they can seek help.

An important part of the psychiatric social worker's job comes when the patient is ready to leave the hospital or institution. The patient is often afraid to face the world he or she ran away from. The caseworker may help by contacting family, business associates, friends, or neighbors and answering any questions they have. If the patient is returning to work, the caseworker may help the patient make arrangements with former employers or employment agencies.

Some patients are not ready to return to a full normal life when they are discharged, and the psychiatric social worker may arrange placement in a sheltered workshop or for continued treatment in an out-patient clinic or with a private counselor. Patients who have been hospitalized a long time may need help and reassurance on how to dress, apply for jobs, or find their way about the city. If they need supervision, the caseworker locates a boarding home or "halfway" house. No matter what the patients' needs, the psychiatric social worker eases their return to life outside hospital walls.

Many psychiatric social workers are employed in child guidance and mental health clinics or in psychiatric divisions of general hospitals. Sometimes they work on an out-patient basis or conduct group sessions for patients. Most psychiatric social workers in the United States and Canada must have an MSW. At present, social work associates who have some training but do not have graduate degrees are hired in state institutions to work under supervision. Many experienced psychiatric social workers are in private practice.

PROBATION OFFICER

Walter Albertson is a probation officer with the Youth Authority of California. No two days are the same for him, and it's not unusual for him to work nights or weekends. Today he's on his way to check a complaint that one of his clients passed a bad check at a filling station.

Walter was assigned to the case before the judge passed sentence on Jim R., who had been convicted of passing four bad checks. Jim was cooperative during his trial, and he had no previous record. The judge thought Jim might benefit from probation instead of going to prison, so Walter was asked to learn as much as he could about Jim to estimate his chances of succeeding.

A social worker discusses a food co-op soon to be set up in this storefront. The boy is a neighborhood worker involved with this project of the People's Development Corporation.

Walter talked with people who knew Jim, discovering that he was out of work and depressed. He wrote the bad checks to buy groceries. Family and friends said that Jim was down on his luck. To Walter, it seemed that Jim deserved a chance, and he recommended probation to the judge. Walter helped Jim find a new job and helped Jim and his wife work out a budget to pay their bills.

Now Jim has violated his probation. Walter wants to know why, so he can decide if Jim should stay on probation or go to jail. If there's hope that another chance will be the turning point for Jim, Walter wants to give it to him. But the line between giving a client a break and having him take advantage of his probation is sometimes hazy, and Walter checks carefully before making the decision.

Walter Albertson had more than a hundred clients at last count. Thousands of men and women who are convicted of crimes each year are placed on probation. Probation may keep a person from further crime, so caseworkers do everything possible to help clients succeed. They supervise where the clients live, their jobs, friends, and activities. They send probationers to alcohol or drug clinics. They have the legal right to detain a probationer and have him or her jailed for up to fifteen days on any technical violation of probation. In short, they can do whatever they feel will help the probationer stay out of trouble. And if their efforts fail, they can advise the court that probation be set aside in favor of imprisonment.

Probation officers are peace agents and are considered part of law enforcement as well as social work. The current trend is toward removing this job from social work status and considering it part of law enforcement. In recent years, the job has been open to women as well as to men. The entrance level is a bachelor's degree, which does not necessarily have to be in social work.

Most jobs come under civil service and carry fringe benefits such as sick leave, vacations, insurance, and retirement plans.

PAROLE AGENT

Parole agents have been described as combination mother, big brother, and cop. They are also social workers and law enforcers, and the work is demanding, difficult, and sometimes dangerous. Its rewards can be great but so can its disappointments.

Parole is the conditional release of a prisoner whose sentence has not been served fully. Any prisoner released on parole is under the guidance, rules, and supervision of a parole agent. Like probation officers, parole agents often begin their work before the client is released. They need a knowledge of social casework, counseling, human behavior, prison conditions, laws and regulations regarding parolees, and the individual's background and history.

Anthony Brentanaro is a parole agent. In his role as "mother," he supervises clients' living arrangements and friends. He visits a prisoner's family before he or she is released to determine if that is the best place for the parolee to go. If Tony thinks the domestic situation may be a contributing factor in getting the offender in trouble, he may decide the client should live elsewhere. Tony is also concerned with his clients' finding and keeping jobs. He calls prospective employers, job counselors, and places of vocational training and tries to line up jobs. If a client gets fired, Tony finds out why, so it won't happen again. People who have been in prison often have personality problems that can be helped by group therapy or individual counseling. Tony knows every program available in his area and sends clients to them.

As "big brother," Tony listens to the parolee's fears,

worries, hopes, and gripes. He checks on clients' activities and discourages any that may lead to trouble. He's not always successful; many clients return to crime. When one is picked up by the police, Tony is notified immediately. He then takes on the law enforcement role of his work. He has first claim on the parolee and can send him or her back to prison by revoking the parole. Tony may overlook technical violations, such as not working or being in bad company, but he takes a hard line with outright violations such as carrying a gun.

Though Tony is a law enforcement officer, he does not carry a gun. Some of his clients and their friends do. When Tony faces a dangerous situation, he has to talk his way out of it. Tony says, "A parole agent needs a silver tongue."

Both men and women work as parole agents. Most jobs are under civil service, and the requirements for hiring and advancement are determined by its rules. The federal government combines probation and parole work under the job title federal parole and probation officer, and the agent handles a caseload of both kinds of clients. A bachelor's degree is required for all jobs in this field; some men and women have advanced degrees.

LAW ENFORCEMENT AIDE

Ann Polanski is a law enforcement aide. She is not, strictly speaking, a social worker, but she has many social-work functions. She answers police calls on family-row-disturbing-the-peace calls. One call brought Ann to a

A social worker (back to camera) discusses plans for a birthday party to be held in a city residential hotel where these older people live.

house where a husband and wife were arguing loudly. The man was drunk, the woman almost hysterical. When she saw the police, the woman began throwing things. Dodging, Ann talked in a quiet voice, asking what had happened and how the fight started. The policemen took the husband into the bedroom while Ann calmed the wife. Mostly, she listened, letting the woman wear out her anger and cry out her misery. Ann sympathized, then suggested counseling at the Project Help offices.

Ann is part of a new kind of social work called crisis intervention. It combines social work with law enforcement in order to reach people who might not otherwise seek help, and who create time-consuming problems for police. Law enforcement aides deal with problems that can be helped by social and mental health services but which come to the attention of the police instead. People often feel threatened when police arrive. Law enforcement aides do not wear uniforms, do not carry guns, and they drive unmarked cars. They work at night and on weekends when most domestic problems occur.

Crisis intervention teams are being formed in many cities as social and law enforcement agencies realize their value in handling calls concerning runaway children, quarrels between neighbors, drunkenness, drug abuse, and family fights. The law enforcement aide needs a good understanding of human nature and modern problems of society. Because the job is still new, no standards or requirements have been set. Each project is different. Most teams have family or mental health counselors on the staff; many also hire trainees with or without college degrees. Trained personnel do short-term counseling in the project offices, and they recommend other community social services when needed. Trainees often work at night, so this is a job where students can get experience while in school.

At present, there is no national organization for people in this work unless they have social work degrees. The best way to learn more about it is to contact either the Youth and Family Services of the welfare department or the police department in your area.

PUBLIC WELFARE WORKER

The largest field of employment for caseworkers is in public welfare programs. These government programs provide services and financial aide to people who cannot support themselves. Aid to Families with Dependent Children, Medicare, food stamps, old age assistance, and similar programs are part of public welfare. Clients include young and old, families and individuals, the sick and the disabled.

In public welfare, a worker can often begin in a clerical job with a high school education and then may move up through the ranks to become a caseworker if he or she gets a college or graduate degree. Some departments provide financial assistance and a leave of absence for workers who wish to acquire professional training, and many require a combination of education and experience for top jobs.

Marie Cartwright began working for a county welfare department as a clerk. She processed forms, handled mail, and typed reports. She was interested in getting ahead, so after two years, she took the civil service examination and was promoted to "intake" worker. An intake worker interviews clients who come to the welfare office to find out if they can get aid. Marie's first client spoke broken English and seemed confused. From his name, Marie guessed that he was Mexican, and she spoke to him in Spanish. He was at ease with his native tongue, and Marie conducted the interview in Spanish. She filled out a form as she asked about his family and his finances. She had him sign release papers so that the department could contact the bank and his employer. Then she told him the office would contact him after the information had been checked.

Marie visited the address the man gave to make sure he lived there. She checked with his employer, who said he had been forced to lay off workers when business was slow; a visit to the bank showed that the client had only the small amount of money he claimed. With the man's need established, Marie then determined how much money and the kinds of aid to which he was entitled. In this case, the family got financial aid, food stamps, and medical assistance.

Marie passed the case on to another worker who met with the client and explained his benefits. This "approved" worker was bilingual also, and made sure the client understood that he had to mail a form to the department each month and to report any changes in his finances. He also had to come to the welfare office every few months so his claim could be checked.

These jobs—clerk, intake worker, and approved worker—exist in all public welfare offices. They are under civil service, and as a rule, a worker must have at least two years' experience and pass a qualifying test in order to move from one job to the next. If a worker has a junior college associate of arts degree, he or she may be able to begin as intake worker.

Many graduate social workers are also employed in welfare departments. They work as caseworkers, like the ones already discussed, with the exception of probation and parole agents. Child welfare workers and psychiatric social workers in public welfare must have master's or doctorate degrees.

Public welfare offers entry into the field of social work for the student who wants to work immediately after high school. Civil service positions provide job security, opportunity for advancement, and good pay.

Information can be obtained through the state department of civil service at the state capitol or from the Public Welfare Department or Department of Social Services in your county. These are listed in the phone book. Canadian public welfare programs are administered by each province under the Minister of Health and Welfare. You can obtain information by contacting the district office of the Ministry of Community and Social Services in your area. Educational requirements vary from one part of the country to another.

CASEWORKER SERVICE AIDE

The number of social services provided by private and public agencies has grown tremendously in the past few years. Social workers have heavy caseloads and can't always spend as much time as they should with clients because time is limited, so some agencies have developed a caseworker service aide program in which paraprofessional aides handle some of the work. Aides learn on the job, or have junior college or trade-technical school educations. In some agencies, these jobs are open to students during summer months. It is an excellent way to get experience or to find out if you will like social work as a career.

Information can be obtained by inquiring directly at public and private agencies in your area. These would be listed in the classified section of the phone book under "Social Service & Welfare Organizations." Your public library can also help you learn the names and addresses of such agencies.

Group Social Workers

Another important kind of social work deals with many people at the same time instead of on a one-to-one basis. Group social work requires the same skills and knowledge as casework, plus the ability to work in a group setting, where people meet personal and social needs through activities with others. These activities range in purpose from recreation to mental health, from social to therapeutic, and the groups range from ethnic to international.

Group social workers must be able to communicate with individuals as well as with the group as a whole. They are coordinators and guides, encouraging the group to develop its own talent and leadership; they make it possible for all members to share responsibilities, work, and fun. They help people get along and settle differences that arise, yet they do not set arbitrary rules. Group workers act as advisers, attending meetings and participating in planning programs. They often teach special skills or counsel members with personal problems. They also help arrange outings and activities with other groups.

As in casework, the group social worker needs a graduate degree to obtain a position of responsibility. However, since group social services are so widespread

A therapy group. The leader is Armand Di Mele, Executive Director of the Di Mele Center for Reconnective Psychotherapy.

and varied, there is more room for those with bachelor's degrees, junior college, or technical school training, and for those without special training.

Private groups set qualifications for their employees, and some consider work experience to be as valuable as formal education. Government programs use many paraprofessionals and accept experience in place of education for promotion. Salaries for group workers are similar to those for caseworkers.

COMMUNITY GROUP WORKER

The Linden Valley Community Center is near the inner city, and several, smoke-belching factories. The neighborhood has many elderly people on pensions, social security, and welfare. There are also low-income families, and recently, young middle-income families in a new housing development. Two years ago, the neighborhood had many problems. Teen-agers spray-painted on walls, youngsters broke windows and hung about street corners. Elderly residents were afraid of being mugged or robbed and spent the days in lonely apartments. In the housing development, families drew an imaginary line between themselves and the "ghetto." The owners of the factories ignored complaints about noise and pollution.

Today, Linden Valley Community Center has helped the neighborhood overcome many of these problems. Stan Free is a graduate in social work, and he helped organize and plan the center. The Community Center has a large recreation room for meetings and social affairs. There is an office where Stan and several volunteers work. There is a day care program for preschoolers, and a program of after-school activities for older youngsters to learn painting, woodworking, and other crafts. The Center also has space for senior citizens to play cards or checkers, talk, or perhaps make items to sell at fund-raising bazaars. Several senior citizens have volunteered as foster grandparents, to be companions to neighborhood children. A social worker from the city mental health center visits once a week to hold group discussions with senior citizens and encourage them to talk over their problems and work out solutions. Stan often sits in on these sessions so that he can follow up with any needed counseling. An action committee of concerned citizens meets at the Center, too. They're interested in cleaning up the neighborhood. They will approach factory managers with a proposal to reduce smoke and noise. They already have the support of a state environmental group, and they are trying to interest their councilman in the project.

The Linden Valley Community Center has become a meeting ground for the entire neighborhood. It is typical of many centers, though not all groups are as large or serve as many different needs as Linden Valley. Some concentrate on certain areas, and may serve special needs of a given population such as senior citizens' groups, Asian-American, Indian, Black, Jewish, or other ethnic groups. Community group workers serve on the staffs of the Red Cross, the YMCA, the YWCA, and similar organizations. "Halfway houses," which help ex-convicts, alcoholics, or drug addicts, also need group workers. Youth groups are also important and will be discussed separately.

Since this work involves a wide range of social services, the community group leader usually has an MSW. He or she may work alone in a center or with other professionals, and also may have the help of paraprofessionals and volunteers. Counseling experience and casework are valuable training for positions in this field.

COMMUNITY SERVICE AIDE

The community service aide is a paraprofessional. In a center like Linden Valley, an aide might supervise senior citizens' activities, helping them locate materials for projects or arranging trips. He or she might organize a job-skills class for teen-agers to teach them how to fill out employment applications or how to act at job interviews. Special talents can make an aide an ideal leader for after-school children's craft classes or an adult community affairs group.

Interested young people from the neighborhood are often hired as aides, as are students who want part-time work while studying for degrees in social work.

DAY CARE AIDE

As Shirley Blackwell enters the bright, sunny room, a two-year-old yells, "Story! Story!" He holds up a book. Smiling, Shirley takes it and sits down. The child scrambles next to her, and half a dozen other eager preschoolers crowd around to listen as Shirley begins to read.

Shirley Blackwell is a day care aide. She is part of the field called social welfare. She works in the day care center of a small midwestern town. The center is operated by the state department of social services and provides child care for mothers who are going to school, working, or those who want to take part in community activities. Shirley reads stories, plays games, and supervises play activities at the center. There are two

This social worker is interviewing a child at St. Luke's Child Psychiatric Clinic in New York.

other aides and a full-time professional social worker on the staff.

Day care centers are not nursery schools and do not necessarily hire licensed teachers. They provide care for young children and encourage them in simple skills and self-sufficiency. Licensed day care centers operate independently and in connection with community centers, schools, and industries. Aides are required to have a high school education and a strong interest in children. Many are students studying for teaching or for social work.

YOUTH GROUP WORKER

Today's neighborhood youth centers recognize the need to serve people in their own community, to go to the source of problems and try to treat causes as well as symptoms. Working with young people is one of the most challenging areas of social work. The problems of poverty, violence, and drugs beset our cities. Crimes that were once considered adult problems are now committed by teen-agers and younger children. The problems of today's youth have become the problems of nations. And the methods of dealing with these problems have had to change with the times; programs that succeed often do so because they are very flexible.

The Neighborhood Youth Association of Los Angeles is one of these successful programs. The NYA serves low-income, hard-to-reach, troubled, and troublesome youths, who are the products and victims of the ghetto and barrio. They range in age from six to eighteen, and all have difficulty dealing with problems of everyday life. Some come because they have heard about the program from friends. Many are sent by probation officers, judges, teachers, or parents. Others are recruited by street-wise staff members who know that youngsters don't always look for help, even though they need it.

Kanata Wilson is the director of the West Area NYA. She holds a master's degree in social work, is a former teacher and family counselor, and she enjoys the variety and excitement of working with young people. She heads a staff of more than a hundred MSWs, BSWs, graduates in psychology, paraprofessionals, part-time workers, and volunteers who work out of a small, two-story house in a racially mixed black and Chicano neighborhood. "Work out" is the key to the success of the program. Staff members spend most of their time away from the center, reaching out to youngsters in their own surroundings and meeting needs where they arise.

Group workers in the NYA have no rules to follow. They need to be creative and flexible. They do whatever works. Crisis intervention is an important part of the job. Staff workers go where and when gangs congregate to try to avert problems before they flare into violence. A counselor may hold a group session on the spot, getting kids to talk about their gripes and trying to find outlets for their anger. He or she may drive the youngsters home or take them somewhere to cool off. Staff members have to be resourceful and adaptable. One worker was supposed to pick up her group after school and take them to a recreational center sponsored by the NYA, but when she arrived, the girls were gone. After some checking, she found them at the home of one of the gang members, all high on paint and glue fumes. The worker took away the dope, aired out the house, then stayed until the girls recovered so that they could have a rap session on the dangers of sniffing.

Schools cooperate with the NYA. Tutoring sessions and talk groups are held in classrooms during school hours. Teachers call the NYA when trouble threatens,

and counselors often go to the school to pick up their kids, removing them from the scene. Kanata Wilson says, "It's usually our kids who are causing the trouble, so things quiet down when they leave." Counselors follow up with counseling to cool tempers and provide alternate behavior. Rooms at the center are open for group sessions at any time.

To solve the problem of writing on walls, the NYA leaders encourage mural painting and publication of a newspaper. To help youngsters see themselves better, the NYA rented video equipment with instant playback. A new Youth TV Workshop was the result. One counselor takes boys to a gym where he coaches boxing. One teaches dancing, another gives music lessons.

Counselors also find runaways and act as go-betweens with schools and courts. Many of the youthful clients are on probation, and workers often drive them to report to probation officers or to appear in court. NYA workers counsel youngsters and parents with home problems, and they operate a twenty-four-hour emergency hot-line as part of the drug treatment program. The NYA also operates a residential home for girls with drug problems. It sponsors a Discovery Room for first- through third-graders in a local school. Supervised by a youth group worker, mothers, social work students, and volunteers help children overcome learning difficulties and turn on to school.

The NYA is a full-program youth organization. In many ways, it is typical of groups throughout the United States and Canada, yet it is also unique. Social workers

Part of a mural showing all the people involved in a community project to clean up their neighborhood. The project was organized by social workers.

who choose youth work may find themselves in programs as varied as this one, or they may work in more limited settings. Youth group workers are employed in churches, community centers, YMCAs, YWCAs, Boy Scouts, Girl Scouts, Camp Fire Girls, and dozens of other similar organizations. Jobs are available at different levels of education and experience, and the worker can select the type of agency he or she wishes to work for. Youth group work is a field that will undoubtedly grow in job opportunities for many years to come.

YOUTH GROUP AIDE

Many paraprofessionals work in youth organizations. Like the Neighborhood Youth Association, most groups offer many activities. While counseling and dealing with special problems is the work of the trained social worker, other jobs can be handled by youth group aides. A street knowledge of troubled young people is needed, and often aides are recruited from the neighborhood or are college students. Busy youth centers also often hire summer workers.

The youth group aide may supervise recreation activities, work as a camp counselor, work on the street with gangs, or teach special crafts or skills. He or she may also assist professional social workers in planning programs or in office work connected with the center.

REHABILITATION GROUP WORKER

Rehabilitation group workers deal with the special problems of the handicapped—the blind, deaf, mentally retarded, crippled, and victims of diseases. They work in prisons, halfway houses, and treatment centers for alcohol and drug addiction. Many hospitals and clinics also have rehabilitation centers for stroke and heart-attack victims. Wherever people must learn to adjust to limitations or to lead new lives, the social worker is an important part of the rehabilitation team.

Gladys Russell is a rehabilitation group worker in a private hospital for children who have bone disorders, crippling diseases, or who have suffered accidents. She works with doctors, nurses, and therapists to help patients and their families overcome the problems of living with handicaps.

"Parents don't want to believe that a son may never walk, or a daughter will never be able to use her arms," Gladys says. "First they shop around for miracles, and when they have to admit there are none, they need someone to help to make the most of the situation."

Gladys Russell holds counseling sessions for patients and families. With the crippled young people, she lets them talk about their fears and anger. "Why me?" is the most frequent question asked, and though there's no answer for it, talking with others with similar problems helps. Gladys encourages discussions on living with handicaps, what kids can do, and how to find substitutes for things they cannot do. One patient's success in handling new leg braces may encourage another to take his or her first step. Gladys also organizes meetings for parents and refers them to medical and social agencies, schools, or institutions.

Dave Schorr is also a rehabilitation group worker, but he works in a center for former drug addicts run by the state Department of Corrections and a large university. He heads a program that trains ex-convicts for social service jobs; his assistant director is one of his graduates. The people accepted into this program have served prison terms for drug-related crimes. In the past five years, only 10 percent have gone back to prison, a dramatic difference from the 50 percent average for the state.

"When you take drugs away from people, you've got to give them something else," Dave says. The center's program offers education and a job future. It accepts only men and women who are off drugs, and it tries to help them learn to live productive lives. Trainees live on the university campus for the first ten weeks of the program. Dave holds frequent group sessions so that the men and women can discuss their fears about the new lives they are trying to lead. Often they're nervous and ill at ease, and Dave has to cheer them up and convince them they can succeed.

Living in rooms on campus gives the students a chance to adjust before going out into the "clean" world. Dave arranges social activities and short trips, often visiting sections of the city where they will live when they move into the second phase of the program, which requires them to be on their own. Dave also counsels on family or marriage problems and arranges tutoring if it is needed. When his people complete the program, he helps them find jobs or get into other schools to continue their education.

There are many drug rehabilitation programs today. Some operate on the street level, where the social worker deals with addicts who are still using. Programs also operate in drug centers, halfway houses, institutions, and prisons. Most employ several graduate social workers and also use paraprofessionals and students. Social workers who hold DSW degrees often head projects of this type, writing up their own proposals and obtaining funds to start new groups. This area of rehabilitation is expanding

Physically handicapped children are often referred to organizations like the New York Philanthropic League where they can enjoy recreation and social contact.

rapidly and offers an excellent opportunity for workable new ideas.

REHABILITATION AIDE

Rehabilitation aides work under the supervision of trained social workers. They are usually hired because of their special ability to relate to the disabled. Many are college or graduate students. With the high demand for workers in social services-health care occupations, many vocational-technical schools and junior colleges offer courses for the student who wants to work in rehabilitation. Some of these are occupational therapy assistant, physical therapy assistant, human services generalist, and human services assistant.

Information on schools offering training can be obtained from the U.S. Department of Health, Education and Welfare or the U.S. Department of Labor. Your school or public librarian will help you find the addresses. You can also get lists of schools from the associations listed in the Education section at the beginning of this book.

WORKSHOP PERSONNEL

Opportunity Workshop employs over a hundred people. Its large workroom hums with activity. Six young men at a bench are fastening colored wires to matching colored terminals of electrical units. Around another table, girls are tying red ribbons to sprigs of holly. Several boys are sweeping the floor and cleaning windows. At one side of the room, girls sit in front of a conveyor belt which carries cardboards advertising a popular glue. Each girl places tubes of glue into slots, and they are emptied onto the passing cardboards. Farther along, other young men run a press that forms a plastic bubble over each tube to complete the packages, which are then put into cartons. From time to time, Carl Pope checks the workers' progress and helps restock supplies. Carl Pope is the only one of this group with normal mentality. The others are retarded young adults who have learned to do simple jobs under supervision.

Opportunity Workshop is a sheltered workshop for vocationally trainable retarded people. For many of its clients, it is the only employer they will ever have. For some, it is a training ground and stepping-stone to other jobs. There are many workshops that serve people with handicaps. Most hire workshop personnel for many different jobs. One worker may spend his time visiting businesses in the area, explaining and selling the workshop program in order to get work the clients can do. One may plan special equipment or methods that the handicapped can use. Another may teach employees how to work on an assembly line or do a good job washing a floor. Some workshops include training in social skills—good grooming, behavior, getting along with others—or basic skills, such as how to use public transportation, count money, or endorse a paycheck.

Sheltered workshops are connected with many rehabilitation programs. The Society for the Blind operates them, as does the Society for Crippled Children and Adults, and the Canadian Rehabilitation Council for the Disabled. The education and training of workshop personnel depend on the special needs of the clients. Working with the blind demands an understanding of what it means to live in a world of darkness; it may also require the ability to read and write Braille. A worker with the deaf needs a knowledge of sign language. Workers with the physically handicapped must be aware of clients' limitations, yet be able to encourage them to put forth their best efforts.

Most workshops have MSWs to counsel clients and

families and to supervise programs and check employees' progress. They also cooperate with other vocational rehabilitation services in testing and placing clients. Some workshops hire MSWs and BSWs, as well as paraprofessionals.

Community Organization Social Workers

As we have seen, every community has health, welfare, recreational, and rehabilitation needs that are met by social service agencies. The number of public and private groups is greater today than ever before, and it is increasing steadily. In large cities, there are often dozens of agencies that offer the same types of service. Even smaller communities often have several similar programs. This can be both good and bad. It is good if the services supplement each other to provide well-rounded care. It is bad if they duplicate services unnecessarily or have to cut activities because of lack of funds, personnel, or facilities. By coordinating efforts and organizing overall programs, social services can be improved and expanded to everyone's benefit.

Community organization social workers make sure needs are met by existing agencies and well-planned programs of expansion. Since planning and directing large-scale social services require a broad background and considerable experience, community organization jobs are sometimes held by DSWs or more typically by MSWs with several years of field and administrative experience.

COMMUNITY ORGANIZER—
POLICY PLANNER AND PROGRAM DEVELOPER

How can a community know if its agencies meet the needs of everyone? How can it be sure that funds are spent wisely? Where will the money come from to support new projects, and who will direct them? These questions are answered by a specialist in social welfare, the community organizer. Community organizers are employed by local community councils, private organizations, national associations, antipoverty councils, or groups working toward specialized improvements, such as urban redevelopment, race relations, housing, or rehabilitation.

Thomas Kanajian works for the United Southwest Council of Los Angeles. As a community organizer, his job is to see that a large area of the city is served adequately by social agencies. After careful study, Tom discouraged the building of a new child care center because several well-established centers were already on hand. He suggested instead that neighborhoods expand a central facility and provide transportation for children in outlying areas. He also found need for a senior citizens' center, because of the growing number of elderly people in the community. Religious leaders were considering a drive to redevelop a slum area. Tom compiled a report on funds available for urban problems, and he invited minority leaders to present ideas at the next council meeting. He contacted labor and business leaders to gain support for a proposed free clinic and to try to get property donated or rented at low cost.

Tom knows all the services of the community. People call him for information, and he supervises a social service exchange that keeps records on everyone served by agencies in the area. The exchange tells social workers what other agencies have worked with clients, so

that they can coordinate efforts instead of working independently.

Tom Kanajian doesn't spend all his time around a conference table. The community is his client, and he often goes out into it. He may take a group of civic leaders on a tour of slums, pointing out which buildings should be torn down, landmarks that can be renovated, and people who must be relocated. He also visits social agencies to study their programs in operation.

Money is always an important factor in social services. Needs can be established, programs proposed, interest stimulated, but without funds to undertake projects, they are doomed. A big part of Tom's job is knowing where and when money is available. He works closely with the United Fund and also helps groups write up proposals for federal grants or to obtain money from private groups.

PUBLIC RELATIONS AND EDUCATION PERSONNEL

No agency can function if those who need its services do not know about it. The task of informing people about the services an agency offers is the work of its public relations and educational personnel. Although these are not social workers, they play an important part in social services.

Marsha Forester is the public relations director for the Community Health Council. Each morning Marsha checks the mail that comes directly to her or is sent by other administrators in the Council. She finds a request to

An architect and members of the community discuss with a social worker the plans for converting this vacant lot to a park and vegetable garden.

use the Council's name as sponsor for a building campaign of a hospital, another from a clinic asking for help in advertising its opening, and another asking her to speak at a meeting of the Women's Club. There are several letters from other community agencies about a proposed mobile health unit and a letter describing a group that wants to join the Council. Next, Marsha and her assistant go over a city-wide promotion program for the mobile health unit. Layouts for a brochure and posters have been made, and they discuss possible changes. They also talk about newspaper releases that will be used in the campaign.

Marsha has a luncheon appointment with an executive from the United Fund office. Then she spends the afternoon visiting a rehabilitation center, meeting with a union leader who wants information on chest X rays for members, and talking with a group of welfare mothers who want increased medical care. When Marsha returns to her office, she collects notes to take home with her so that she can organize a presentation on plans for Health Awareness Week.

Marsha's job is typical of public relations in community organizations. Her work changes constantly as new programs require new approaches and contacts, and established programs demand follow-up and fresh ideas to keep the public interested. A good public relations person is always on the lookout for better ways to inform the community about the agency's services, goals, and accomplishments. It is not necessary to have a degree in social work for this job; a background in advertising or business is helpful.

FUND RAISER

Many social service agencies belong to central fund-raising organizations, such as community chests or the United Fund, which put on yearly drives to raise money.

These groups help finance member organizations, but they do not support them completely, so agencies often have their own fund raisers to secure additional money. Some agencies raise all their own funds, and these usually have a fund-raising department.

Fund raising is specialized work. Many groups compete for the public's dollars, and it takes careful planning to make an appeal attractive and convincing. Fund raisers first determine how much money is needed. They consider where and how it can be raised. They analyze the community to estimate how much will come from business, other groups, and the public. The next step is to help develop a program that will present the campaign to the people, and finally they solicit volunteers to carry it out. They may need men and women to run a carnival or block workers to ring doorbells. They need supervisors to work with volunteers and collect money. Getting pace-setting gifts and endorsements from prominent citizens can make a big difference in the success of the campaign, and fund raisers write letters and telephone and visit people personally.

Once campaigns are under way, fund raisers make sure they run smoothly and that interest doesn't lag. If results are behind goals, they have to think up new ways to encourage donations. Even after the campaigns are over, the fund raisers' work is not done. They have to write letters of thanks, perhaps hold victory dinners, and cooperate with public relations people in announcing results.

Every fund raiser must be completely familiar with the operation of the agency. He or she has to be ready to answer questions, give facts and figures, and talk about services. The fund raiser does not need a degree in social work but in business administration or a similar area. Experience in management or accounting or in the administration of social service agencies can be extremely helpful.

Researchers

Federal bureaus, private foundations, and social service agencies sponsor many research projects aimed at uncovering, understanding, and treating social problems. Researchers estimate costs and evaluate techniques being used or develop more effective ones. They also organize and operate pilot programs to test theories.

A research project in Los Angeles led to the development of a Crisis Intervention Team to work with law enforcement officers in responding to domestic disturbances. Its success spurred a study of the possibility of using the same techniques for neighborhood disputes. Researchers in Minneapolis developed a pilot model-city program for a low-income area with a high crime rate. The pilot center was a clearinghouse for complaints and for social service referrals; it was also a place where residents of the community could get answers to questions about housing, schools, medical, and legal matters.

With the need for new programs in treatment of drug addiction, juvenile delinquency, and racial tensions, the emphasis on research has grown in recent years. Research projects range from short-term studies to aid in developing neighborhood programs to lengthy surveys of the problems of an entire city. Graduate programs of study in social work include courses in research, and

A senior citizen hot-lunch program in Sweet Home, Arkansas.

3833

students are required to complete independent research project. An MSW or DSW is needed for most research positions, though some of the supervised work may be carried out by those with less education.

Administrators

The work of administrators cuts across all areas of social work. Every agency needs executives to plan, handle finances, and direct operations; most have an administrator, administrative assistant, and several department directors. Each has specific duties, with the administrator responsible for the entire operation. In many agencies he or she also writes proposals for funding, is in charge of hiring and firing personnel, and sets agency policies.

The director of a neighborhood youth organization checked her calendar and read off the notes for one day: the housemother for the residential facility quit—interview two new applicants for the job; received notice that a former employee is suing for the cost of two surfboards; another case involving damage to a worker's car is scheduled for court—talk to lawyer; contact list of volunteer sources—need twenty people to help with sum-

**Working out a program at Aspira,
a New York educational program
for high school and college students.**

mer programs . . . all this in addition to her regular tasks of correspondence, phone calls, and reports.

Administrators are usually MSWs or DSWs with many years of experience. They must be able to handle a wide variety of tasks, situations, and people. Top executives usually earn at least $20,000 a year and may earn $30,000 or more.

Teachers

There are more than four hundred undergraduate study programs and schools of graduate social work in the United States and Canada. The demand for qualified teachers is high. Associate degree courses and paraprofessional training in junior and community colleges also need teaching personnel.

Colleges and universities require a master's degree for most entry teaching jobs, with preference being given to applicants with doctorates. Some institutions have teaching-aide positions available to graduate students as a form of financial assistance. This experience is excellent in helping the student decide if he or she enjoys working in education; it may also help the student secure a job after acquiring a degree.

Teachers and consultants are needed within agencies and service programs, too. Social workers often conduct classes for other professionals, such as law enforcement or school personnel. They work in medical schools, theological seminaries, and with public and mental health units to train staff members in social services that affect their clients. Teachers are also in demand with agencies of foreign countries that are developing social welfare systems or adapting new ideas.

Teaching salaries begin at $4,800 a year for teaching assistants, and range from $12,000 to $30,000 for instructors, assistant professors, and professors.

Private Practitioners

Madelaine Rush has a private social work practice. Her specialty is family and marriage counseling. After obtaining her MSW, Madelaine worked for twelve years with various agencies. She was a family counselor with Citizens' Aid; she was on the staff of a large community center where she worked with families of school-age children with behavior problems; for eight months she was the resident counselor at a home for delinquent girls. She enjoyed all these jobs but wanted the independence of being self-employed. She felt she could do the most good in family counseling since she believed that the roots of most problems begin in the home.

Madelaine's office is in a suburban business district. Her clients are mainly middle to upper class and prefer the personal attention Madelaine offers to seeking help at an agency. They have the same kinds of problems Madelaine dealt with before she opened her own office, but they come by appointment, sometimes as often as once a week. As in all counseling work, Madelaine encourages clients to think through problems for themselves. She works closely with psychiatrists and psychologists, who often refer patients to her, and she arranges consultations with specialists in child guidance or play therapy as they are needed. A married couple may sense that their conflict stems from disagreement over the behavior of a child and that the child needs professional help.

Private practice requires at least an MSW, a broad background of experience, and a reputation of achievement. Clients are referred by other social workers and agencies or hear about the consultant by word of mouth. It often takes a long time to build a practice, and the consultant must expect to have an outlay of cash for office expenses to get started, but income can also be high. Many private practitioners make $25,000 to $50,000 a year. Private practitioners work in the fields of family, marriage, child counseling, medical, psychiatric, and rehabilitation social work.

Jobs Abroad

The need for social services is worldwide. Federal, international, and voluntary agencies sponsor programs of direct service, development, and training in many countries. All levels of social workers can find employment with the Agency for International Development, Peace Corps, State Department, and military services. The United Nations, UNESCO, World Health Organization, and the Organization of American States sponsor technical assistance programs in which social workers play an important role. Among the voluntary agencies that work overseas are the Red Cross, International Social Service, and American Friends Service Committee.

Foreign assignments include working with displaced persons, in health centers, aiding disaster victims. There is also a need for trained social workers who can help develop human resources. Many countries are establishing their own welfare services in response to growing need. Consultants, teachers, and social workers are in great demand.

Looking at the Future

Wherever you want to work—city, town, or distant country—there may be a job for you in professional social work or one of its closely related fields. There are more social service programs today than ever before, and there are jobs for workers at all levels of education. Agencies and schools actively recruit from ethnic, racial, and religious backgrounds to find workers with close ties and special understanding of minority problems. The field needs tried-and-true methods and creative new ideas. And it's a career where you can test your interest before committing yourself. There are many volunteer jobs in social services; by working in one or in several, for a summer or after school, you can find out if this career appeals to you and whether or not you're suited for it.

Economic conditions affect social service programs greatly. During times of economic recession, the need for programs is often greater, while the money to put them into operation is harder to obtain. Sometimes the result is that fewer jobs are available at professional levels and more people compete for them. But it also may increase the need for workers—in public welfare, for example—or encourage new programs which employ a large proportion of paraprofessionals to work under the supervision of trained social workers. The availability of jobs also varies from one part of the country to another, since many programs depend on financial aide from the states as well as private and federal sources. At present, government cut-backs in Canada are seriously affecting community college programs in social services, and job opportunities for graduates are limited.

Social work may not be for everyone, but if you're one of the outgoing, outreaching people who choose it, you can look forward to an interesting and satisfying future.

Professional Organizations

American Friends Service Committee
1501 Cherry Street
Philadelphia, Pa. 19102

American National Red Cross
17th and D Streets, N.W.
Washington, D.C. 20006

American Public Welfare Association
1155 16th Street, N.W., Suite 201
Washington, D.C. 20036

Canadian Association of Social Work
55 Parkdale Street
Ottawa, Ontario K1Y 1E5

Canadian Red Cross Society
95 Wellesley Street E.
Toronto, Ontario M4Y 1H6

Canadian Rehabilitation Council
for the Disabled
242 St. George Street
Toronto, Ontario M5R 2N5

Child Welfare League of America
67 Irving Place
New York, N.Y. 10003

Council of International Programs
for Youth Leaders and Social Workers
1001 Huron Road, E.
Cleveland, Ohio 44115

Day Care & Child Development
Council of America
1012 14th Street, N.W.
Washington, D.C. 20005

Drug Abuse Council
1828 L Street, N.W.
Washington, D.C. 20036

Family Service Association
of America
44 East 23rd Street
New York, N.Y. 10010

International Council
on Social Welfare
345 East 46th Street
New York, N.Y. 10017

International Unit
Social & Rehabilitation
Service/DHEW
330 C Street, S.W.
Washington, D.C. 20201

National Association of the Deaf
814 Thayer Avenue
Silver Springs, Md. 20910

National Association
for Retarded Citizens
2709 Avenue E, East
Arlington, Texas 76011

National Association
of Social Workers
1425 H Street, N.W.
Washington, D.C. 20005

National Council on Family Relations
1219 University Avenue, E.
Minneapolis, Minn. 55414

National Council
for Homemaker-Health Aide Services
67 Irving Place
New York, N.Y. 10003

National Council of Senior Citizens
1511 K Street, N.W.
Washington, D.C. 20005

National Easter Seal Society
for Crippled Children and Adults
2023 West Ogden Avenue
Chicago, Ill. 60612

National Federation of the Blind
218 Randolph Hotel Building
Des Moines, Iowa 50309

National Federation
of Clinical Social Workers
c/o Wright Williamson
7979 Old Georgetown Road, Suite 312
Bethesda, Md. 20014

National Rehabilitation Association
1522 K Street, N.W.
Washington, D.C. 20005

Ontario Association
of Children's Aid Societies
663 Yonge Street
Toronto, Ontario M4Y 2A4

Peace Corps
ACTION
806 Connecticut Avenue, N.W.
Washington, D.C. 20525

Society for Hospital Social Work
Directors
840 N. Lake Shore Drive
Chicago, Ill. 60611

United Way of America
801 N. Fairfax Street
Alexandria, Va. 22314

Index

About the Author

Marilyn Granbeck is a prolific writer of both adult and young adult mysteries, novels, and non-fiction. Before starting her career as a writer, she was a research chemist. The author became interested in social work as a result of personal experience. For eight years, she worked as a volunteer with the Welfare Department of Hennepin County, Minnesota.

When she can take time off from writing, Mrs. Granbeck likes to travel. A trip to the Yucatan originally stimulated her strong interest in Mayan civilization.

The author has four children and lives in Agoura, California.